Note to the Reader

A Field Guide to the Heart is unique in that it is part poetry book and part journal. Because we believe in the power of poetry to inspire reflection and creativity, we have included pages for you to respond. May you find solace and joy in doing so.

To the women in my circle of love ... my amazing Mom and trio of wonderful sisters — Lisa, Jaqueline, and Patty

~ GH

In memory of my brother and both of my beloved fathers. And for my mother and sister, whose memories are lost, so I keep them for you. I will love you all to the stars and back until the end of my days.

~ RKD

GEORGIA HEARD & REBECCA KAI DOTLICH

A FIELD GUIDE to the HEART

POEMS OF LOVE, COMFORT & HOPE

CONTENTS

8 — **HOW FRAGILE THE HEART IS**

10 — A FIELD GUIDE TO THE LOST
Georgia Heard

12 — IMAGINE
Rebecca Kai Dotlich

14 — NOT TODAY
Georgia Heard

16 — NOTE TO THE UNIVERSE
Rebecca Kai Dotlich

18 — FLIGHT
Georgia Heard

20 — WHAT BECOMES OF US
Georgia Heard

22 — WHEN I WAS A GIRL
Georgia Heard

24 — LAMENT
Rebecca Kai Dotlich

26 — THEY WERE NOT SIMPLY NAMES (A FOUND POEM)
Georgia Heard

28 — BLUE SILENCES
Rebecca Kai Dotlich

30 — EVENSONG
Georgia Heard

32 — WHAT WILL SURVIVE US?
Georgia Heard

34 — REFLECTIONS

38 — THE MORNING OF MY CHOOSING

40 — THE MORNING OF MY CHOOSING
Rebecca Kai Dotlich

42 — WE HAVE BEEN THROUGH THIS BEFORE
Georgia Heard

44 — REMINDER JOTTED IN A JOURNAL
Rebecca Kai Dotlich

46 — HINGING ON NOTHING AND EVERYTHING
Rebecca Kai Dotlich

48 — 5 SMALL THINGS TO DO TO CHASE AWAY THE BLUES
Rebecca Kai Dotlich

50 — GRAVITY
Georgia Heard

52 — CHANCES ARE
Rebecca Kai Dotlich

54 — SIGNS
Georgia Heard

56 — ON EVENING WALKS
Rebecca Kai Dotlich

58 — NIGHT PRINTS
Georgia Heard

60 — REFLECTIONS

64 — A QUIVERING OF WINGS

66 — A QUIVERING OF WINGS
Georgia Heard

68 — NEW BEGINNINGS
Rebecca Kai Dotlich

70 — THERE WILL ALWAYS BE
Rebecca Kai Dotlich

72 — STAR STUFF
Georgia Heard

74 — THE CEREMONY OF GIVING
Georgia Heard

76 — PROMISE TO MYSELF
Rebecca Kai Dotlich

78 — A SHATTERED PIECE OF TIME
Rebecca Kai Dotlich

80 — CARVING MY OWN LANGUAGE
Georgia Heard

82 — SOMETIMES I DREAM
Rebecca Kai Dotlich

84 — AN INVITATION FOR WORDS
Georgia Heard

86 — REFLECTIONS

INTRODUCTION

Let everything happen to you: beauty and terror. Just keep going. No feeling is final ... Nearby is the country they call life ... Give me your hand.

— Rainer Maria Rilke

Poetry has always been there for us in times of need and in times of love. When emotions run deep and raw, it is often poetry that has the power to comfort and speak truth to what yearns to be awakened inside. In moments of sorrow and struggle, many of us have turned to the wisdom and peace that poetry can offer. And we discover, time and time again, how remarkable it is that poetry bridges what can be a wide divide between human beings.

In the spring of 2020, we slowly realized how much we needed one another. We missed so much — a hug from a friend, a sister, a parent, grandparents, grandchildren, even the ritual of a simple handshake. We missed the comforting hum of voices in our neighborhood coffee shops. After sheltering in place for months, we each experienced profound

loneliness, sometimes boredom, and often grief as we fought off despair. Our hearts ached with each countdown of death, both in our own families and beyond. And then we heard the desperate calls of *I can't breathe*; the world felt like it was exploding and imploding at the same time as we grieved and protested the anti-Black and anti-Asian racism that surrounded us. We woke up to the world's, and our own, anguish and heartbreak. The universe shrank, and we needed something to make it expand again.

    Two poets. Two friends. Reaching out to each other, deciding to put hearts on paper, we discovered a strength and resilience we didn't know we had. This is how this book came to be. Not a field guide to identify and name things of this universe — birds, stars, flowers — but a field guide to explore and name what we've lost, what we've found, and what fills us with love, comfort, and hope — *A Field Guide to the Heart*.

    A Field Guide to the Heart is part poetry book and part journal. Because we believe in the power of poetry to inspire reflection and creativity, we have included pages for you to respond. We hope that you find solace and joy in doing so.

    — Georgia Heard and Rebecca Kai Dotlich

HOW FRAGILE *the* HEART IS

Sing like the little, brown sparrow. Sing to me now if you can, through a sky gone dark.

— Catherine Bowman

How do we find hope when we feel surrounded by loss and uncertainty? How do we endure the absence of a loved one? Or bear the long battle with an illness and have the courage to keep going? How do we find a new way to love the world when we are heartbroken and when we find ourselves in need of encouraging words, shared stories, inspiration, inner strength, and fortitude? One blueprint for this journey is through poetry.

    The poems within this section try to find a way to share how it feels to be lost, to grieve, to worry, and how we all try, as in the poem "Imagine," to "hold tight." We often go to sleep and wake up with heavy hearts and disappointments. But in "Not Today," there are mornings we make decisions to "stay curled up in the clouds" and to chase away the "hungry hours/ gnawing into my dreams."

Loss is a uniquely personal experience, and yet it can also be a universal one, as in "Note to the Universe," in which we find ourselves longing for the way things were, for the "lazy days in museums" and the "litany of months... missed." Whether it's a beloved mother who sometimes forgets our name but still feels the missing, as in "Lament," or imagining strangers' lives in "Flight" or the child who grows up and leaves us, as in the bittersweet "What Becomes of Us" — we share empathy for others' experiences and lives. As in all losses and tragedies, "They Were Not Simply Names" reminds us that we live with empty chairs and rooms and the profound hurts that find us struggling with reasons and doubts and acceptances.

  We know that we all engage in similar rituals, as in the poem "Blue Silences." For instance, we might "light a candle and mark/a calendar of days" of people, of lives, and of endings. In "Evensong," we say the name that sparked a movement that brought us hope. And oh, how we wonder and dream of what was, what might have been, and what will endure in "What Will Survive Us?" Loss and grief are deeply sobering and exhausting, and yet we come out of it. There is no other way, really, than the eventual way out. And when we do, we realize, as in the poem "When I Was a Girl," how very "fragile the heart is."

A FIELD GUIDE TO THE LOST
Georgia Heard

Printed on the first page of my notebook are the words:

In case of loss, please return to:

_____

Phone:

_____

Address:

_____

This notebook is my field guide
to the lost. To what's lost
in me.
If I follow the trail of words
it will lead me home.

reflections

IMAGINE
Rebecca Kai Dotlich

Imagine the wavers, the watchers, the wishers,
the calmers, the doubters, the dreamers,
the wonderers, the worriers, the whisperers.
Imagine them all, early in the morning,
late in the day, in the middle of the night;
they are at their windows.
Imagine all the words: *Hold tight, I miss you,*
this will end, we'll be together, Happy Birthday,
I'm praying for you, I'm thinking of you,
I'll drop off flour on the porch, and a tin of cookies.
Thank you, you're welcome, I hope you feel better,
can you feel this kiss on your cheek?
Soon. Soon. I'll see you soon.
I'll make you a poem. I'll make you a picture.
I'll knit you something in shades of blue.
I am at my window, waiting.
Please come to yours...

reflections

NOT TODAY
Georgia Heard

This morning, I pull
the quilt over my head
and stay curled up in the clouds.

I don't want to feel
the hungry hours
gnawing into my dreams.

I don't want to read
the grocery list of *should haves*
when all the shelves are bare.

I don't want to water
the dry flowers when a drought
has turned my world into desert.

I don't want to hear
the reedy song of hope
hidden somewhere in the back of my throat.

I don't want to hear it —
not today.

reflections

NOTE TO THE UNIVERSE

Rebecca Kai Dotlich

Give me back
those lazy days in museums,
coffee shops, bookstores;
those long and lingering
conversations on park benches,
those crowded sidewalks
and easy trips to the grocery
for crisp apples and cheeses
while breathing in scents
of lemon and mint,
rambling aisle to aisle without
floor arrows, and
give me back
those carefree hours
that held more serenity than worry.
Give me back the litany of months
I missed, the loved ones lost,
give me a rain check
for joy.

reflections

FLIGHT
Georgia Heard

Looking down
through an oval window, a bridge
over a snaking green river.

I imagine the lives below
in the miniature houses
dotting the fields.

A woman stands at a kitchen sink,
stares at a bare
tree in her small, fenced-in yard.

Lying on his bed, a teenage boy
traces stories of lost
friends in a constellation of ceiling cracks.

From his driveway, a man listens
to the distant roar of a plane,
wishes he could get away.

I hear the faint sound
of a bird's wings flapping —
little bursts of heartbreak.

reflections

WHAT BECOMES OF US
Georgia Heard

Today, I touched the top
of my son's head —
a buzz cut, all the curls gone
it felt downy like when he was a baby.

Hold onto it, they say,
it goes fast.

But what they don't tell
you is no matter how tight
you hold on, they leave.

You write books,
move from house to house,
city to city,
and you learn to live
in your world without them.

reflections

WHEN I WAS A GIRL
Georgia Heard

we took turns
asking silly questions.

> *Would you rather
> eat an Almond Joy or a Slurpee?*

> *Would you rather
> live in a tent or a treehouse?*

At some point
our questions turned serious.

> *Would you rather
> lose your brother or your sister,
> your mother or your father?*

We were young.
None of us had lost anyone yet.

We didn't know then
how fragile the heart is.

reflections

LAMENT

Rebecca Kai Dotlich

Shell
    after shell
        after shell . . .
I string salmon-colored, smallish shells
onto a cord of twine, for my mother,
for my mother, for when she misses,
she misses the sea;
this will be her necklace of
slapping waves and
heartbeats of harbors,
shell after shell after shell
for my mother, when she misses,

when she misses me.

reflections

THEY WERE NOT SIMPLY NAMES
(A FOUND POEM)

Georgia Heard

Toward the end of May in the year 2020
one hundred thousand people died.
They were:

> A conductor with the most amazing ear.

> A bonfire builder.

> A man whose backyard birds ate from his hand.

> A grandmother who was known for Greek chicken and stuffed peppers.

> A father who called his children "sweet pea" and "pumpkin."

They loved baseball.
They loved seeing the full moon.
They were more than names on a list.
They were us.

(This found poem is a moment in time from *The New York Times*, Sunday, May 24, 2020.)

reflections

BLUE SILENCES
Rebecca Kai Dotlich

You might feel the rain
of tender breaths and hardy sighs;
of faces, names and notebooks.

Between blue silences
and beneath tumbling gray skies
we cry for us, for them,

for those we never knew.
We light a candle and mark
a calendar of days, an invisible tabulation

of the wronged and the heartsick,
the mourned and the mourner,
the grandparents who never came home,

the empty chairs
          and endings.

And we cry.

reflections

EVENSONG
Georgia Heard

When I saw the news,
his cheek pressed to the street,
blue knee on his neck,
I asked,
didn't he plead
I can't breathe?
Didn't he invoke
his mother's name in prayer
to deaf ears and hardened hearts?
A dark cloud
loomed over the city for days
as echoing chants rang out,
saying his name.

reflections

WHAT WILL SURVIVE US?
Georgia Heard

My 93-year-old mother asks,
what will survive us?
Does she mean
when the world ends,
or when we end?

I close my eyes
and imagine
what I would miss
when we're no longer here,
to name the things I love in this world.

White lilacs,
peonies in a chipped vase,
honey bees.
A blue teapot with a bamboo handle,
a faded photo of an old friend,
summer dresses and a red scarf,
moonlight paving a dirt path,
letters sent and forgotten.
A 1000-piece puzzle of the blue
earth with pieces missing.

reflections

how fragile the heart is

REFLECTIONS

REFLECTIONS

THE MORNING *of* MY CHOOSING

Without darkness, nothing comes to birth, as without light, nothing flowers.

— May Sarton

The poems in this section are about repairing, seeking ways to heal, tuning in and raising our antennae to hopeful signs in the universe — signs that help us reconnect with ourselves and the world. But repairing and healing are not passive acts: healing happens naturally, often unknowingly, with time, but we also make the mindful decision to choose to live...to fight, to struggle to feel hopeful again.

Sometimes healing can be as simple as intentionally taking notice of and praising the "ordinary things," as in "The Morning of My Choosing," and to celebrate "the lost letter/found again," as in "Reminder Jotted in a Journal."

Children naturally relish small things, and in our busy and complicated grown-up world, we can learn from the wisdom of children to notice "dandelions braided into love chains" and the other small things described in "Hinging on Nothing and Everything." This kind of slowed-down, intentional focus is almost devotional and is what poets do — to see and name the ordinarily invisible things — and in that we may find peace and hope.

Especially when we're struggling, observing the natural world can bring relief and take attention away from ourselves as it connects us to a larger world. Sometimes we choose to read what we observe in the natural world as something more than it first seems — perhaps even something divine, as in "Signs" and "We Have Been Through This Before." If our antennae are tuned in, we ask ourselves what, if anything, are "trees sewing cold nights/and storms into rings" trying to tell us? Could they be delivering messages from beyond our immediate understanding if we listen carefully, only then finding a way to hear them?

Or in another interpretation of signs, we notice "light posts and fence posts" in "On Evening Walks" as not divine signs but as symbols of "hard work" and "repairing."

In "Gravity," loss is transformed into something profound as Isaac Newton grieves for his mother and conceives of this symbolic description of longing, and perhaps even love.

After loss, after pain, we can never replace what's lost exactly, as "Chances Are" describes, but it doesn't stop us from searching.

We can also find ways out of sadness by thinking outside the box, by finding joy in ways that aren't rational or logical, as "5 Small Things to Do to Chase Away the Blues" invites us to do.

And finally, we end this section with "Night Prints" by searching for our own words of repair and allowing our deepest thoughts and hopes to be tucked under our pillows, to be released into the universe and into the night. For who knows where dreams might take us.

THE MORNING OF MY CHOOSING

Rebecca Kai Dotlich

This is the morning
of my choosing.
I will not cater
to calendar or clock,
but instead pass time
praising the porch step,
the clover,
the jangle of chimes,
the tree frog.

I will notice small things,
wise things,
ordinary things,
while sending a true
and tender prayer
into air...
on this,
the morning of my choosing.

reflections

WE HAVE BEEN THROUGH THIS BEFORE
Georgia Heard

Are you listening? Do you hear
waves unfolding tight fists
outstretched towards you?
We have seen dark storms.

Are you listening? Do you hear
trees sewing cold nights
and storms into rings?
We have dug our roots in deep.

Are you listening? Do you hear
birds weaving threads of song
into nests of sadness?
We have been through this before.

reflections

REMINDER JOTTED IN A JOURNAL

Rebecca Kai Dotlich

Let me not forget to celebrate.

Not just the birthdays
and anniversaries
but all the unexpected and
mundane moments;
the snow day,
the lost letter
found again,
the scent of oranges.

Times are hard
and full of worry
just waiting beneath
the errand,
the restless nap,
the wrong turn
around the sharp corners
of the day, so in some small way

let me not forget to celebrate.

reflections

HINGING ON NOTHING AND EVERYTHING

Rebecca Kai Dotlich

I should be writing about living and dying
and all those days between; about the grieving
and the heartbroken, about protests
and school policies and vaccines,
about history and sea discoveries
and celestial findings.

Instead ...

I write what's scrawled
on the cave of my childhood heart;
the blue Schwinn,
dandelions braided into love chains,
the stack of old comic books,
pastel sandals and cherry popsicles.

reflections

5 SMALL THINGS TO DO TO CHASE AWAY THE BLUES

Rebecca Kai Dotlich

Sing so the birds will know you.
Ring silent bells.
String beads of rain.
Tell secrets to clouds.
Write poems to plums.

reflections

GRAVITY
Georgia Heard

The particles of everything on Earth attract.
        The farther away a body is — the weaker the gravitational force.

I imagine you standing at a window
        looking out at a blackening sky

traffic lights flicker red green yellow
        swinging over the ghost of 14th Street

and me 2000 miles away.

In Newton's equation I'm m_1 and you're m_2.

They say he discovered gravity
        watching apples fall from a tree.

But it wasn't the apples that gave him the idea —
        it was his mother dying.

Gravity pulls humans   toward each other.

reflections

CHANCES ARE
Rebecca Kai Dotlich

I lost something once.
It might have been an umbrella
or it might have been a friend.
Either way, I felt the losing.

One kept me dry
in a pouring rain
and one just *kept me*.

I find myself searching now.
For something to replace
that umbrella, that friend.

And every day is the day
I never find it, exactly.
But nothing,
nothing can be *exactly*.

reflections

SIGNS

Georgia Heard

Today, as I turned
the corner of my street
two yellow butterflies
circled in a figure eight.

A cardinal sang in a branch.
On the sidewalk, I spied
the silver feather of a small songbird.
An oncoming storm rumbled on the horizon.

At home, dirty dishes pile in the sink,
a ticker tape of fear crawls
across the flickering screen,
and unpaid bills weigh on my desk.

It's as if a door has been opened
and I can see into what's possible,
signs from an invisible world
speaking a language
I'm struggling to learn.

reflections

ON EVENING WALKS

Rebecca Kai Dotlich

I study light posts and fence posts
and the crooked trail of cracks in the sidewalk
because they remind me of the beauty
of hard work, and how they all have a time
for breaking apart
              and for repairing.

reflections

NIGHT PRINTS
Georgia Heard

I collect words
to tuck
under my pillow.

Words like —
    tender
    patience
    beloved

At night I press
them into sleep.

When I sleep
I release them into the sky.

reflections

REFLECTIONS

the morning of my choosing

REFLECTIONS

A QUIVERING *of* WINGS

Hope has conspired with the wind and blown away the demons of despair.

— Maya Angelou

Has there ever been a time when you felt flat inside, and even numb, when suddenly you're walking across the room or pouring milk into a cereal bowl or washing your face, and you look up and see yourself, *really* see yourself, in the mirror — when you're doing something seemingly insignificant but out of nowhere and before you know it, you feel a quickening inside, a blast of what feels like hope? It may lighten the heaviness of your day and your heart for a moment, or it might compel you to pick up a pen and write. Stunned by both brokenness and beauty, we found ourselves doing just that. Writing about our own joys and journeys, we also were able to map out gratitude along the way, often urging each other to breathe, notice, laugh and heal.

The poems in *A Quivering of Wings* are about that moment when inspiration and hope conspire, and you can't stop singing, writing, and feeling that elusive and yearned for "taut thread of hope" that comes with "New Beginnings." Then you look around and understand that "There Will Always Be" "the burble/of streams, the charm of birdsong,/the whisper of wind" and that "sadness is not forever."

The poem "Star Stuff" is about feeling connected by the essence and components of stars — connected to loved ones both alive and gone and with family and strangers alike. "The Ceremony of Giving" portrays a kinship the speaker feels with her mother, and all women, who "know the secrets of life, of how to love" through the simple and ceremonial act of baking.

If and when sadness returns, we will try keeping the "Promise to Myself" to "sit under a tree" while "dreaming of spired rooftops."

And we write of how from sorrow and grief comes love, as in "A Shattered Piece of Time" and "Carving My Own Language," where we find both abstract and literal ways to speak about what is broken — discovering that words themselves have healing power and a promise of renewal, and how we sometimes "dream of carving a new life" in the poem "Sometimes I Dream." Eventually, we come to believe that our inner voices and our deep desire to share words are the ultimate force for hope and healing, and so we end this section, and the book, with "An Invitation for Words." An invitation to express your truths, your burdens, and your steadfastness from your own unencumbered heart.

A QUIVERING OF WINGS
Georgia Heard

In the beginning, small poems
lay still and silent inside your hearts.
If you listened carefully,
you might have heard
a quivering of wings.

Then, from the corner
of your eye, you spied
a flutter or two —
poems slowly unfolding,
delicate silken wings.

Poems appeared everywhere.
Hovering over desks,
hanging from ceilings,
tips of noses, tops of heads.
It was difficult to get any work done.

Now, your poems
fly free. You fold words
into memory. Poems:
small butterflies raised, watched,
let loose into the world.

reflections

NEW BEGINNINGS

Rebecca Kai Dotlich

For everything, there is a beginning.
It often comes from a place of knowing,
or of remembering,
or of emptiness.

Then come the familiar middles:
the dandelion, the daisy, the butterfly.
Woven in is the clothesline, the creek
the taut thread of hope, and the globe that turns
with a skyful of languages.

Then comes the end and it will always be that, the end
of a story, a song, a storm;
                        the end of winter,
                                      the end of grief.

reflections

THERE WILL ALWAYS BE
Rebecca Kai Dotlich

There will always be the waves
rushing in and tumbling out;
the promise of the moon, the bronze
of the morning sun.
Sadness is not forever.
But let hope be.

Let it sit by seaside towns
and wander in cities.
Let it linger
in schoolyards and shipyards
and farmlands.

Let it call to you with a healing chant
and the constant chime
of the clock.

There will always be the burble
of streams, the charm of birdsong,
the whisper of wind.
Sadness is not forever.
But let hope be.

reflections

STAR STUFF
Georgia Heard

A boy once told me,
We are made of star stuff.
I imagined bits of shine
broken off from stars inside us.
He meant, we are made of divine ingredients —
calcium in our teeth, iron in our blood,
every atom in our bodies crafted
in the kiln of long-dead stars.
You. Me.
Those we've never met,
might never know,
in cities and towns we've only read the names of —
kids playing soccer barefoot in the streets of Rio,
a girl riding her bike to school in Accra,
even the boy in Orion, Alabama
gazing up at the spattered canvas of night —
all of us plaited together by stars.
On starry nights
mothers, fathers, friends we've lost
wink at us.
We are made of stars,
we dazzle.

reflections

THE CEREMONY OF GIVING
Georgia Heard

I am becoming my mother
as I turn the scrappy biscuit dough
onto the floured kitchen counter,
reverently humming the choir of my hands.
Ploughing and kneading soft flesh
my hands sticky and coated with flour.
I gently flatten the dough with my palm,
folding each side to the center,
my fingers worn and bent like my mother's.
How many women have played
this same tune for untold years?
We know the secrets of life, of how to love,
patting out rounds,
careful not to overwork the dough,
keeping it soft and crumbly,
cutting each biscuit, making sure not
to twist the cutter and seal the edges,
rerolling the scraps (these will be less tender).
My sleeve is dusted. My heart is dusted
with the ceremony of giving.

reflections

PROMISE TO MYSELF

Rebecca Kai Dotlich

I will sit under a tree,
gaze at a puzzle
of sky between branches;
contemplate the fragility of twigs
while dreaming of spired rooftops
and clocks ticking in small villages
near countrysides full
of bluebells and cowbells ...

tomorrow.

reflections

A SHATTERED PIECE OF TIME

Rebecca Kai Dotlich

I accidentally dropped it once.
It splintered into a hundred pieces
or more; glass shards and porcelain,
small parts and gears.

My grandfather picked up
the shattered piece of time
and tenderly held it to the light.

A lump caught itself
in my small throat.
He held my face in calloused hands
and kissed my forehead,

and I was introduced
to love.

reflections

CARVING MY OWN LANGUAGE
Georgia Heard

There is a crack in everything,
that's how the light gets in.
　　　　　　　　　　— *Leonard Cohen*

When I was a girl
I saw a crack in the world
a clean, flat line where Earth meets sky
where sun dims into darkness —
a break that lives beneath the surface of all things:
glass, walls, bones, teeth.
I knew that someday when I grew up
I would gather that light
to carve my own language.

reflections

SOMETIMES I DREAM

Rebecca Kai Dotlich

of being a carver;
smooth wood cupped in my hands
and a carving tool, silver and curved

poised and ready
while the gloss of sun
swaddles the window in August.

And so I dream of carving
a scalloped shell, a curled leaf,
the tiny beak of a bird.

I dream of carving a new life, too,
but instead, close my eyes and breathe;
settle in to the familiar,
as some serene voice whispers

just be.

reflections

AN INVITATION FOR WORDS
Georgia Heard

Treat them like a guest in your own house.
Tell them to make themselves at home.
Light a candle.
Leave the door unlocked,
the porch light on.

reflections

a quivering of wings

REFLECTIONS

REFLECTIONS

GEORGIA HEARD is the author of 18 books, including *The Woman in this Poem: Women's Voices in Poetry* (Plumleaf Press), and her poems have been published in numerous anthologies, magazines, and journals. She received an MFA in poetry from Columbia University, and travels the world giving workshops and keynotes on writing and poetry. Georgia has been a poet since childhood, and believes in the power of poetry to help restore our sense of well-being and find balance in our lives. She lives in South Florida with her husband and family.

To learn more about Georgia, check out her website www.georgiaheard.com, and follow her on Instagram @georgiaheard1 and Twitter @georgiaheard1.